About the Book

The first Seminoles were Indians of several tribes who fled from the white men into Florida. After a while, the white men tried to make them leave their homes there, too. Osceola, a young chief, would not give up his people's land.

The Seminoles and the soldiers fought for many years. Between battles, the Indians hid in the swamps. They had few guns and little food. Finally, Osceola and his followers lost the war, but even today there are Seminoles living in Florida.

Here, in an easy-to-read presentation, is the story of Osceola, brave leader of the Seminoles.

A SEE AND READ
BEGINNING TO READ BIOGRAPHY

OSCEOLA

by Marion E. Gridley

Illustrated by Lloyd E. Oxendine

G. P. Putnam's Sons • New York

OSCEOLA

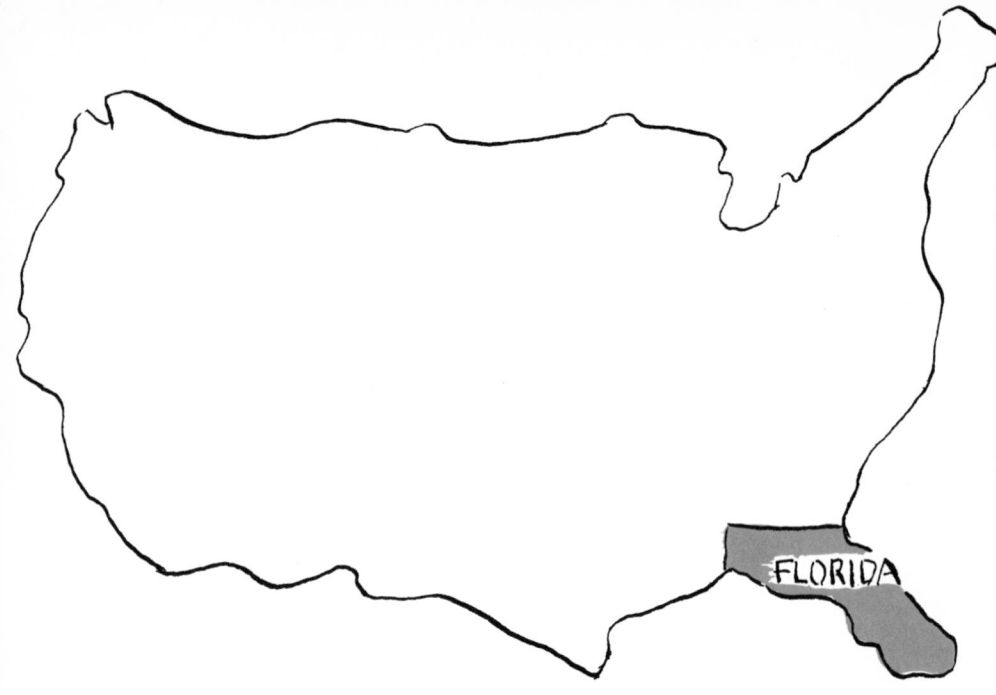

A little Creek Indian boy came with his mother to live in Florida in 1808. No one knows what his name was then. Later, when he became a young man, he was called Osceola. It means "Black Drink Singer." The boy had been born in Alabama. His father was an Englishman.

In Florida, the boy and his mother lived with the Seminole Indians.

Seminole means "run away." The Seminoles were Indians who had run away from their homelands farther to the north. There had been fighting among their old tribes and trouble with the white settlers. Some Indians were killed. Many were forced off their land, so they had come to Florida to form a new tribe.

Osceola's home was an open
shack with a palm leaf roof. It was
called a chickee. In front of the
chickee was the fire where
Osceola's mother cooked. At one
side, there was a small garden. The
Seminoles grew corn, beans,
pumpkins, and squash.

Osceola's chickee and others like
it were built in an open clearing on
a riverbank. Around the village
grew huge oak trees. Moss hung
from the branches.

As Osceola grew older, he learned the skills of a man. He could pole his dugout canoe along the river. And he could hunt the animals in the forest and catch the fish in the river. There was always plenty to eat. Osceola and the other Seminoles were seldom hungry. It was a good life.

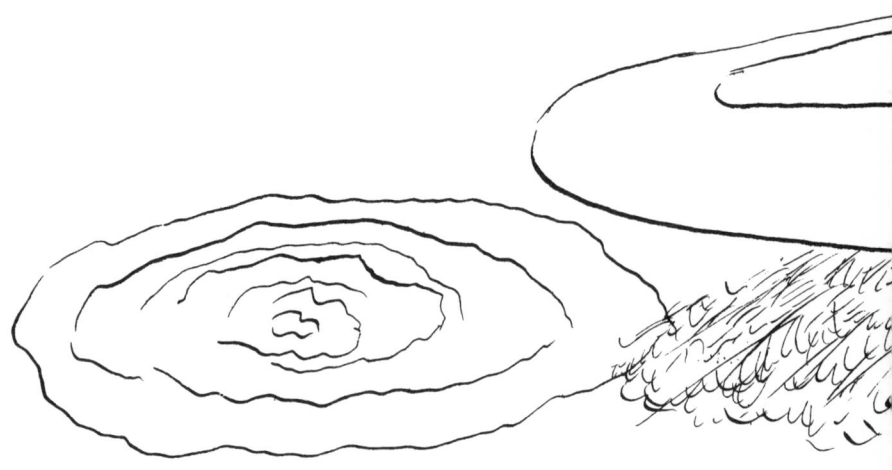

Spanish people lived near the village. The Seminoles traded with them for guns, cloth, kettles, beads, and coffee. Sometimes they traded for other things they could not make or grow themselves.

One day a strange Indian came to the village. He had startling news.

"The Spanish are leaving Florida," he said. "They have sold the land to other white men. They are called Americans."

"But the land did not belong to the Spanish," the Seminoles said. "It is our land. We have not sold it to anyone."

The Seminoles were troubled. They wondered what would happen next.

Osceola listened as the man
talked. He wished that he was a
grown man so that he could speak.
I know what I would say, he
thought. *This is our land. No one
will drive us away. That is what I
would say.*

But the Americans wanted all of
Florida for white people. They did
not want the Indians to stay. "We
need this land for our settlers," the
Americans said.

By the time Osceola was grown, the Americans and the Seminoles had met many times. Always the Americans brought a paper.

"Sign it!" they ordered. "Give up your land. Say you will leave and we will give you money. There are good hunting lands across the Mississippi River. No white people live there. We will help you to go."

But most of the Seminoles said, "No!" They would not sign the paper. Only a few chiefs were willing to do so.

"It is best for the Seminoles to leave now," they argued. "If we wait too long, the white men will send soldiers to make us go. Then we will get nothing. We will lose everything."

It made Osceola sad to hear the chiefs talk. "A man fights for what is his," he told his mother. "The Seminoles should be men."

Osceola spoke to the other Seminoles, too. "Fight, fight!" he urged. "I will never leave Florida. I shall fight. Do not give in."

The other young men said they, too, would fight. They would help Osceola.

When the Seminoles and the Americans met again, Osceola came to hear what was said. He was not a chief and he had no war honors. But he was looked up to as a leader.

General Wiley Thompson spoke for the Americans. "Your chiefs have promised many times to leave Florida," he said to the Indians. "Still you are here. You must go *now*."

One old chief, Micanopy, shook his head. "Eleven years ago, we put our names to a paper," he said. "We gave you much land. You promised we could keep our homes. Why don't you keep your promise?"

Osceola jumped to his feet.

"That paper was a trick," he cried. "You have broken that promise. We will not leave here. We do not say tomorrow, or next year. We say never. We will never leave."

"I speak only to the chiefs," General Thompson replied. "You are not a chief. You are *no one*."

But the Indians cried out,
"Osceola speaks for his people. He
speaks for us." And the old chief
Micanopy nodded that this was so.

General Thompson spread a large
paper on a table. It was yet another
treaty.

"This is a new promise paper," he
said. "President Jackson will not
give you any more time. If you do
not promise to leave soon, soldiers
will make you go. Sign!"

Some of the older men who felt
it was wise to leave went to the
table. They made cross marks on
the paper where their names had
been printed. They could not write.

Osceola, too, went to the table. In his hand he held a knife. He stabbed it into the table. The paper shook where the knife stuck.

"This is the only way I will ever sign a treaty with white men," Osceola cried. "We do not go!"

The Seminoles followed him back to their village.

Not long after this, Osceola was captured by soldiers. He fought like a wild cat. But he was dragged to the Army fort and put in chains.

"Will you sign the treaty?" the soldiers asked Osceola. He knew that to sign was the only way to go free.

"If you let me go, I will sign," Osceola answered. The Americans trusted his promise. They told him that he could leave the fort but he must come back in five days. He must bring his people so that they could see him sign.

Osceola came back in five days. He brought all of his followers with him. They watched in silence as he put his mark on the paper. But the mark had no meaning. Osceola had promised only to make it. He had not promised to go away. He turned to his people.

"Let us go to the swamp," he said. The Seminoles knew that he meant to fight.

Now all the Seminoles agreed not
to leave Florida. "If we are to die,
we will die here," they said. "We
will kill any Seminole who does not
fight with us." The Seminole War
began. It was the longest and the
bloodiest Indian war of all. The
Indians fought only soldiers.
Osceola had said they would not
make war on women and children.
Settlers' homes were burned, but
women and children were seldom
hurt.

The Indians raided forts and
settlements. They attacked Army
supply wagons. Each time, they
struck quickly and then raced back
to the swamp. There they were
safe. The soldiers could not follow
them.

Deep in the swamp, the Indians were hidden. Tall cypress trees grew close together in the water. But canoes could slip between them. High grass covered the trails. The Indians moved as silently as panthers. The children played quietly. There was no shouting, laughing, or crying. The people spoke in whispers. The only sounds were the hoarse whumpf of an alligator, the cry of a heron, or the calls of the other swamp animals.

The Seminoles were few and weak, but they knew what they had to do. They fought against guns, although they did not have many of their own. They fought against cannons, although they had none. In one of the first battles, they killed many soldiers. Osceola told them to keep on fighting.

"We have won this battle, but there will be others," he said.

Osceola did not stop, even when he was wounded. He caught a bad sickness and was never well again. But he did not give up.

More and more soldiers came to
Florida. The Seminoles lived in the
swamp, a lost, hunted people.
Soldiers tracked them down with
dogs. Some Indians were captured
and sent to the West.

Osceola knew now that the
Seminoles could never win. They
were only a few against an army.
He sent word to the American
generals that the war would end if
his people could stay in Florida.
But he was always refused. The
Americans still said that the
Seminoles must go.

Two years after the war began, some of the Seminole chiefs gave up. Their people were hungry. They had no time to hunt, and they could not plant gardens in the swamp. There was little powder for the few guns. The chiefs led their people to Fort Brooks. From there they would go on to the West.

But Osceola would not let this happen. He had only two hundred warriors, but he led them in an attack on Fort Brooks. They captured the Indian chiefs and took them away. The rest of the Seminoles slipped out of the fort and went back to the swamp. The fighting began once more.

Osceola led his people back and forth across Florida. Many were killed. Many were sick. All were hungry. At last, he sent word to General Hernandez.

"I will meet you under a flag of truce," he said.

A flag of truce is a white flag.
While it flies, the people who are
fighting one another can talk
together in peace. Afterward, each
can go safely back to his own
camp.

When General Hernandez and his
troops came to the meeting place,
Osceola stood under the white flag.
He was thin and he looked tired
and sick.

"Will you leave Florida?" the
Americans asked.

Osceola shook his head. "We want
peace," he said. "We will give you
all of our land. We will stay in the
swamp. But we will not leave
Florida."

The soldiers did not leave.
Instead, they captured Osceola and
the other leaders and took them to
Fort Marion. It was an old Spanish
fort in St. Augustine. The soldiers
put the Indians in a cell with a
high window.

Brokenhearted, Osceola would climb to the window and look out through the bars. The Indians starved themselves until they were thin enough to squeeze through and escape. But Osceola refused to go with them. He knew that he was dying.

Osceola longed to go home. Instead, he was taken to Fort Moultrie in South Carolina. His spirit was broken and it was only a short while before he could no longer speak.

One night, he motioned that he wished to see his family and the other Seminoles who were in prison. He wanted to wear his warrior clothes. With great pain, he got to his feet. First, he put on his shirt, his leggings, and his moccasins. He pinned feathers in his hair. Then he stuck a knife in his belt. It was the same knife that he had stabbed through the promise paper.

Osceola shook hands with the
Seminoles and the Army officers
who had come into the room. He
motioned good-bye to his two wives
and his children. Then he painted
half of his face red, the mark of a
warrior. When he could no longer
stand, he lay on his bed and held
his knife on his chest. With a sigh,
he closed his eyes. The great
Osceola was dead. He was only
thirty-four years old.

The Seminole War lasted eight more years. When it ended, most of the Seminoles were sent away. But Osceola's people stayed in the swamp. They were too few to worry the government. Like their leader Osceola, they never gave up. Their great-great-grandchildren live in Florida today.

Osceola was greatly admired by his people. He was admired by the white people, too, even though they fought him. Twenty towns, three counties, two townships, one borough, two lakes, two mountains, one state park, and one national forest are named for him. Twenty-two states have places named Osceola.

Osceola fought to save his homeland. He fought fairly and bravely. He had promised his people that they would not leave Florida. His promise was not broken.

Key Words

alligator	general	skill
cannon	heron	soldier
canoe	homeland	swamp
capture	Indian	trade
chickee	knife	treaty
chief	panther	tribe
cypress	promise	trick
dugout	seldom	truce
force	Seminole	warrior
fort	settler, settlement	wound

Places

Alabama	Fort Moultrie
Florida	Mississippi River
Fort Brooks	South Carolina
Fort Marion	St. Augustine

Other See and Read *Books About Indians*

Crazy Horse *by Glen Dines*
Pocahontas *by Patricia Miles Martin*
Pontiac *by Marion E. Gridley*
Sacajawea *by Virginia Frances Voight*
Sequoya *by Ruby L. Radford*

The Author

Marion E. Gridley has long been interested in Indian culture and is an adopted member of two tribes — the Omaha and the Winnebago. She and her parents founded the Indian Council Fire, a national Indian-interest organization of Indian and white membership, and Miss Gridley has served as its executive secretary since its beginning. In addition to having written a large number of books about Indians, Miss Gridley is the editor and publisher of *The Amerindian,* a bimonthly information bulletin about Indians. She has written *Pontiac, The Story of the Navajo,* and *The Story of the Iroquois* for Putnam. The latter book won a second place award from the National Federation of Press Women in 1970.

The Artist

Lloyd Oxendine is a young Cherokee artist. Born in Pembroke, North Carolina, he studied art at the University of North Carolina, the Art Students League, and the Columbia University School of the Arts. His work has been exhibited in shows and galleries throughout the country, and his paintings have been acquired by many private collectors. At present, Mr. Oxendine is organizing an exhibition of contemporary American Indian art for the Metropolitan Museum of Art in New York City. The artist lives in New York with his wife and young son.